First Facts®

Expert Pet Care

CARING for Cats

A 4D BOOK

by Tammy Gagne

Consultant:
Jennifer Zablotny, DVM
Member, American Veterinary Medical Association

PEBBLE
a capstone imprint

Download the Capstone app!

- Ask an adult to download the Capstone 4D app.
- Scan the cover and stars inside the book for additional content.

When you scan a spread, you'll find fun extra stuff to go with this book! You can also find these things on the web at www.capstone4D.com using the password: catcare.27391

First Facts are published by Pebble
1710 Roe Crest Drive, North Mankato, Minnesota 56003
www.mycapstone.com

Library of Congress Cataloging-in-Publication Data
Names: Gagne, Tammy, author.
Title: Caring for cats : a 4D book / by Tammy Gagne.
Description: North Mankato, Minnesota : an imprint of Pebble, [2019] |
    Series: First facts. Expert pet care | Audience: Age 6-9.
Identifiers: LCCN 2018018362 (print) | LCCN 2018019549 (ebook) | ISBN
    9781543527513 (eBook PDF) | ISBN 9781543527391 (hardcover) | ISBN
    9781543527452 (paperback)
Subjects: LCSH: Cats--Juvenile literature.
Classification: LCC SF447 (ebook) | LCC SF447 .G227 2019 (print) | DDC
    636.8--dc23
LC record available at https://lccn.loc.gov/2018018362

Editorial Credits
Marissa Kirkman, editor; Sarah Bennett, designer; Tracy Cummins, media researcher;
Laura Manthe, production specialist

Photo Credits
Capstone Studio: Karon Dubke, 5, 9; iStockphoto: fridayphoto, 17, kali9, 15; Shutterstock: 5
second Studio, 7, absolutimages, 6, AlinaMD, Back Cover, 24, Axel Bueckert, 21 Bottom Right,
DenisNata, 19, ekmelica, Design Element, Eric Isselee, 21 Top, everydoghasastory, 21 Middle,
Jorge Casais, 16, Kasefoto, 4, liudmila selyaninova, 11, Oksana Kuzmina, 3, Peter Wollinga,
23, rawcapPhoto, 20, tatianaput, 13, TatyanaPanova, 21 Bottom Left, Utekhina Anna, Cover,
Vasek Rak, 8, Vicki Vale, 18, Zoran Photographer, 12.

Printed in the United States of America.
PA017

Table of Contents

Your New Pet Cat

Cats are popular pets. Playing with these furry animals can be great fun.

Many cats and kittens are in **shelters**, in need of a good home. You must learn how to care for a cat before taking one home. Owning this animal is a big **responsibility**. Your family will need to choose a cat that is right for your home.

FACT

There are different types of cats. Some cats have short hair and others have long hair.

shelter—a place that takes care of lost or stray animals

responsibility—a duty or a job

Supplies You Will Need

You will need a set of bowls for food and water for your cat. Your cat will also need a litter box and litter.

Cats often dig their claws into things. Toys and scratching posts can stop cats from using their claws on your belongings.

Many cats **shed** year round. Brushing your cat will help keep hair off your clothes and furniture. Try to do this once a day.

FACT

Make sure to buy a cat carrier. It will be helpful for taking your pet on trips outside your home.

shed—to lose hair

Bringing Your Cat Home

Keep your pet in one room for the first day or so. This can make it feel more relaxed. You can then let it explore your home.

Many cats do well with other animals. But owners must always be careful. Some cats have a strong hunting drive. They may try to eat smaller pets such as hamsters or birds.

Some adult cats can sleep up to 16 hours a day!

What Does a Cat Eat?

Your pet needs food made especially for cats. This food contains **vitamins** that keep cats healthy.

You can feed your cat canned food, dry kibble, or both. Fresh drinking water is as important as food. Cats who eat wet food do not need to drink as much water.

Canned food can **spoil** if it is left out too long. Owners must place leftover wet food in the refrigerator.

vitamin—a nutrient that helps keep people and animals healthy

spoil—to become rotten or unfit for eating

Cleaning Up After Your Cat

Cats are very clean animals. They do not need baths unless they roll in something dirty or smelly. Cats clean themselves with their tongues. This can cause **hairballs** in the cat's stomach.

A cat's litter box should be scooped every day. You'll need to change the litter at least once a week. Most cats will not use a dirty litter box.

hairball—a ball of fur that collects in a cat's stomach; hairballs are made of fur swallowed by a cat as it grooms itself

FACT

Regular brushing helps prevent hairballs.

Visiting the Vet

All cats need a yearly checkup with a **veterinarian**. You should also take a cat to the vet if it gets sick or hurt.

Spaying and **neutering** prevents cats from having kittens. It can be done once a cat is four months old. This step lowers the number of animals in shelters.

Your cat may need shots at its vet visits. These help keep your pet healthy too.

veterinarian—a doctor trained to take care of animals

spay— to operate on a female animal so it is unable to produce young

neuter—to operate on a male animal so it is unable to produce young

Life with a Cat

Cats can be mighty playful. They may bat at toy fishing poles. Others chase balls that make noise. Toys often make cats run, leap, and **pounce**.

Some cats snuggle with their owners. But a little playtime each day is good for your pet. Exercise helps keep cats healthy.

pounce—to jump on something suddenly and grab it

Cats pretend to hunt while playing.

17

Your Cat Through the Years

Cats go through many stages of life. Kittens have lots of energy. They need plenty of playtime each day. Adult cats are usually calmer. But they can still be playful.

Cats can have a long **life span** when well cared for. Most cats live about 15 years. Some have even made it to 20 years.

Older cats may eat less and sleep more than younger animals.

life span—the number of years a certain kind of plant or animal usually lives

Cat Body Language

How a cat behaves tells people a lot about what it is feeling. These animals meow when they want to eat or play. Purring often means a cat is happy. Hissing is a sign the animal is scared or angry. A cat that wags its tail is likely showing interest in something nearby.

Types of Cats

Devon Rex

Some of the most playful cats are:

- Devon Rexes
- Manx cats
- Munchkins

Manx

Some of the smartest cats include:

- Abyssinians
- Siamese cats
- Turkish Vans

Abyssinian

Siamese

21

Glossary

hairball (HAIR-bawl)—a ball of fur that collects in a cat's stomach; hairballs are made of fur swallowed by a cat as it grooms itself

life span (LIFE span)—the number of years a certain kind of plant or animal usually lives

neuter (NOO-tur)—to operate on a male animal so it is unable to produce young

pounce (POUNSS)—to jump on something suddenly and grab it

responsibility (ri-spon-suh-BIL-uh-tee)—a duty or a job

shed (SHED)—to lose hair

shelter (SHEL-tur)—a place that takes care of lost or stray animals

spay (SPAY)—to operate on a female animal so it is unable to produce young

spoil (SPOIL)—to become rotten or unfit for eating

veterinarian (vet-ur-uh-NER-ee-uhn)—a doctor trained to take care of animals

vitamin (VYE-tuh-min)—a nutrient that helps keep people and animals healthy

Read More

Bacon, Carly J. *Cat Care: Nutrition, Exercise, Grooming, and More.* Cats Rule! North Mankato, Minn.: Capstone Press, 2016.

Gardeski, Christina Mia. *Cats: Questions and Answers.* Pet Questions and Answers. North Mankato, Minn.: Capstone Press, 2017.

Meister, Cari. *Cats.* My First Pet. Minneapolis: Bullfrog Books, 2015.

Internet Sites

Use FactHound to find Internet sites related to this book.

Visit *www.facthound.com*

Just type in 9781543527391 and go.

Super-cool stuff!

Check out projects, games and lots more at
www.capstonekids.com

Critical Thinking Questions

1. What supplies will you need to have in order to care for your cat?

2. Why is it important to watch your cat when smaller animals are nearby?

3. What does it mean when your cat wags its tail?

Index